MIRRORS

MIRRORS

POEMS BY

Twixt

PINYON PUBLISHING
Montrose, Colorado

Cover Art "5 de dezembro" by Paulo Oliveira Ramos

"Infinite Infinitessimals" and "Beyond Numb" first appeared
on the Waywiser Press Website.

First Edition: July 2021

Pinyon Publishing
23847 V66 Trail, Montrose, CO 81403
www.pinyon-publishing.com

Library of Congress Control Number: 2021939034
ISBN: 978-1-936671-77-9

Contents

WITNESS-PROTECTED

It's good looking in a peaceful looking
direction, nothing in particular
besides near infinite existence in
action, of the visible, felt and heard,
is there to record.

COMING CLOSE TO THE INFINITE

Infinite, only in that we're pinpricks,
space, which by looking a person projects,
comes to be less infinite, yet still is,
being so far, so close to it.

THINGS WILL COME AS THEY ARE

Things will come as they are, essentially,
standing out, in the distance we view from,
as separate, unique with apartness,
common to the greater universe.

WHAT A DIFFERENCE MAKES

What difference would a different universe
make in this to which we're wired in tight,
if we made contact? Well I imagine
time would fail to integrate with either
to the other, and attempts would grind gears
in clocks. Or, an amalgamatory
reconciliation would make a rate
common to the two, to make the two one,
neither would win, what we'd have's doubles.

A COUPLE UNIVERSES AWAY

Just a couple universes away
things aren't all that different, life's like life
as we live it; in the in-between, though,
the formality of distance forbids
such talk, withdraws its support; things that float
float off.

INFINITE INFINITESIMALS

In the infinity of what I think
pelletable to the smallest measure
within the field of compressible space
where atoms and their parts make tiny marks,
as light turned me on I've oft gotten off.

REAL OBJECTS

Real objects, at their different distances
from me, large or small as their size expounds
or distance explicits, I find are hard
in fact, to touch, and to conception soft.

BEYOND NUMB

Outside, the concrete, the ground, minerals,
light, the running water and reflective
puddles, why even the forceful shadows,
consume the drug of not being alive,
and though some move, none are aware of it,
none take pleasure in their painless leisure.

ROADWAY

Mechanical metal carrying lights
with directional shine, shining on rain
and the sparkles rain imitates, and shapes
it aggregates, dominoed and drooled to.

A STRETCH OF BURGEONING

The optically blue, optically tickly
flowing flowering, the glabrous polished
fruits, the powder-blue blue-powder glaucous
perfect plums, the nummular sunshine dimes.

LIGHT & LACK

Blue can be seen in black or next to it
much as yellow seems to appear in white
or be left as a surface where white falls.

THE LIGHT

The light has disavowed this direction
and let the force of its evidence fail,
so that, not what's black, but what isn't, is
black, with without-light without.

AN EVENING PINK

An evening pink and a zooful of birds
break explanatory obvious rank
with permanent to all appearances
rock-obvious cliffs.

COLOR

Each color stakes its individual
claim, dismissing what people have called it,
where they have, and how they have compared it.
I am thinking of Color A; I know,
when I see it, it will be different.

BY THE EYE-SCOPE

What I see as orange appears in leaves
in quick conversions from previous greens,
and by the juices released that release
me, internal chemical pleasure pours.

ONE DAY IN AUTUMN

Fall colors fall from sprayed-on crowns down,
and develop from the outside leaves in,
or the whole tree, for some of them, converts
its color overnight; furthermore sky
allows clouds self-aggrandizing whites,
and clouds in turn bend to blue ultimatums.

IMBIBITION

Trees are sucking water, quiet diet.
The silence of the minerals of earth.
What sound there might be, reaches nobody.

FLOATS

There are leaves at the edges, the margins
and the hollows, the spread sheet surfaces,
and some leaves temporarily afloat
on a waft, dock, dropped, but by gust, reboat.

STORM DAMAGE

Force struck and broke structure, and structure scarred
over; a cicatrice of bark, where barked,
left its bossed mark.

THE HIGHER POINTS OF TREES

Precise, up to the neck, then top-heavy
with topiary, engineered to flail
in significant weather about. So,
so slow to catch on quick is what the tops
show when shook.

In the daily dapple birds duly move
dollying by on wheels of energy;
they themselves are dapple-items,
and the dapple-results of shadows passed.

THE PHYSICAL'S PHYSICAL

There are the various non-awareness
inevitable items which make up
the land, physically participating,
perma-frostily, heatedly, blasé:
water's loose grip on just about everything
set in its way, an instant for-instance;
the strong shadow-government of the sun,
semi-selective in its abuses;
the tourniquet that the wind turns leaf-bleeds
off with, which twist with the twists ...

SOFT SHAPE

Existence briefly at rest in the
performance of its essence which is
restless.

DOING THIS

Motions move me and in response I lift
whatever is in me to do this up;
sometimes, starlight dispatched from ages back
is what I contact; other times, items
of white developments, temporary
each to each, endlessly recurrent.

MOTIONS

In the cool unusual, leaves raffle
and flex believable phenomena,
which with comparisons eyesight assists,
place to place in space from a point that's fixed.

SWIRL

Puff-particles, and their compadres puff-
gusts, in their actions with acrobatic
twists display erratic schoolyard conducts,
within and out of touch.

DOING JUSTICE TO IT

I don't know how to do justice to it
but a direct production of the sky
has traveled miles and miles to get to me
in a blue form with drifting white items.

OF THINGS AT REST

Of things at rest in their existences,
such opposites of bubbles, viz. fizz, as
say cloudy white items, those few whose floats
blue sky supports, I see, seeing grow, seed
flow.

CLEARING

Coagulatory clouds cloy the parklands
and green leaves drip clear slivery streams
clear to the ground onto scattered tree leaves
separation has browned. New winds then remove
the passageway clots and open the throat
of the quick way out.

SKY CLOUDS

A decent amount of the thoroughfare
accounts for itself in big white items
that make their way through the blue in glimpses.

UPWARDS OF UPWARDS

Quietly and without moving much clouds
without raising dust relocated; sky
squeaked (like window glass squeaks clean) blue, washed
off with millions of looks by points of view.

WILLING ARRIVAL

I arrive in a state of willing mind
for the coming individuation
of the water from the land; and the clouds,
their intercontinental balletic
molecules, test the urge.

LIVE STREAM

A brown butterfly flew in and flew out
of the building's hospitable lobby,
and inapropos I thought of how creek
water in sheets folds on over small rocks
and flings itself out with white-bubbled lips
from minor dips.

BLEED

The creek leaks along its thin incision
in the hills and gains not loses liquid.

THE LIGHT AND THE WATER

Due to (whatever science might fill in)
bright light turns the water white where bubbled,
or (equally valid view) the water
bubbles light within, which makes it whiten.

ENOUGH RAIN

Enough rain to turn green brown greenery
leaves its drops of imperfect brief lenses
full of light's bends as well as its gems bright
atop top foliage.

CLEAR TRICKLES

Clear tintinnabulatory trickles
collect where its possible, then escape
at high level reachably hit, leaving
after-trails of no-slime in dirt.

CREEKY

The net example of all the trickles
tributary to the will of the creek
is something so many critters follow
and objects obstacle.

As single and as multiple motion
the divisible/indivisible
stream, in that manner felt suitable,
over the dead engines of some stones, strews
its juggernauted path.

People notice the water spillover
(which starts as a palm and ends as fingers)
makes symbols of things that work themselves free,
gloving up around the small obstacle stones
and their enormous cousins a plastic
of glass.

AFTER A RAIN

The more water the faster, the louder,
the less twist to the flow path, the greater
conduction of anything caught on up
in where it's going: that direction wins.

WET SNOW

Surprise surprise a few very first flakes
drape-shaped flop flat wet and liquefy back
to rain. And the so-called light just like lights
past has settled its shine on the slick side.

SPILLINGS

Water froths frost, its replacement-sponsored
falls' fallings-off practiced exactly—
clearly taxis white opacity—

CASCADILLA

A diminished frizzle of clear brittle
froth runs over and off sort of a shelf,
and that this glass phase of fluid finds
frees.

UPLAND BOAT

Through the hull of the gorge in its keel-vee
the creek is tossed and tosses, leaving bilge
pools and ochre sediment deposits,
sluicing and sloughing its way to the stern
seacock lake/exit alluvium depot.

AERIAL VIEW

From above I see the stream espaliers
twigs of trickles upon rocks-as-trellis,
I see routes of retrunk rush down reroutes
I know will delta to spread wet roots out.

THE STRONG FORCE

The strong force in the forced space entertains
the rock resistance, slipping over it,
a molecule thick of slick and rapid
contact, which takes a few atoms with it.
So siennally stained with elements
it's gained and clearly contains it swidgets,
where it's let, smidgens by the millions.

BRUTE BROKE FORCE

Roar, sienna; millions of smithereens
in a smidgeon each of rainfall runoff,
loud and coughy, the coffee colored streams
collared in ravines—drain-collections rich—
these light to look at hard to hear are deaf.

SURF PIECE

The surf rises and slap-flattens on sand
which rises and comprises land or slips
its grips individually, flipping
over backwards into the sea.

BOAT SWIMMINGLY DRUNK

Swimming with doll fins in the dark ocean's
black & froth back & forth, antagony
abounds in the waves, needy needles knife
the sea-skin at points, pointing to rain, spray
digital with light, yes-like and no-not,
green-kelp purtenance in ships' abature.

PROPELLER OPERATOR

I'm living life in the wake of water
propelled to a digital brilliance
by twist, the gurgling torque outfits,
I stand one hundred percent behind
the scudding van, my future's fan.

ADRIFT

I forgot which was which and which wasn't
at sea in the ocean that I lighthouse,
the push-science guys try oomph to get through
and a few do, a few triumph, they reach
shore. I am never shore.

AN OLD WAY OF THINKING

My assumptions were blown up and exposed
more than once in their go's at survival
and had to be left in revised formats
or left for death and replaced for good
to be done with; some clung, though they were wrong,
fossils of wrong turns right life took.

WHAT'S TRUE FOR YOU?

What's true is not on page one hundred and
that, lost in the way a person had thought
to write who wrote. The truth is objective,
even objectionable objects rate,
not ultimate truth but beyond debate.

THAN

As the wider and wider the concept
the more skeletally narrow the brittle
marrow, that gets to that point that it snaps,
gets, so off the concept in a blue streak
of science the thinker jets.

DETERMINATION

Funny how when you make up your own mind
and conclude with a formal decision,
people jump on it, want to gussy it up
into something taking the direction
they like; something about it strikes them as
hittable.

TRAITS

People are reluctant to let be known
what they are known by unless they know you,
there's a back-&-forth parity to traits
that's a trait of traits, for those who use them.

QUEST SHUN

Who or what would I want to keep touch with
and touch with what touches that audience—
or would I want to change that audience
or would I want to change audiences,
only I can answer, and wonder why.

MIRRORS

None look back at me for identity,
they look forward to someone of interest,
therefore I lack a self that attracts looks,
it appears; I do not appear outside
of in mirrors.

AMNESIA

Of all the things that were always there, there
were a few that disappeared in nowhere,
so as to escape notice that they had.
These are what fill your lack of memory
with a feeling of compactness and flaw.

THE TRAPPED

Some have been too long in a spot to leave
by their own leave, and believe it's their wish
to persist, which it isn't, it's their wait.

TIME CHANGE

Out of the ocean of now, to new nows,
something like light has swum, and something like
-wise has found its wiggle-way in.

EXPANSION

Previous to my capacious thought
with its envelope of good intentions,
fluffy white puffs of puffy white items
in the blue, in acknowledgements of blue,
made welcome to any thought of that size,
so that I had to adjust up the mind.

GETTING GOING

I've a thing going for getting going
off in the upward I set my sights on,
free of the sweep sleep dream pattern program,
over the obstacles which can be jumped,
out to, into, up at, clarity-full,
involved, free, absolved, free, and furthermore.